RICK BROADBENT *Illustrated by* ALEXANDER MOSTOV

SUPER SPORTS STARS WHO ARE CHANGING THE GAME

WALKER BOOKS
AND SUBSIDIARIES
LONDON • BOSTON • SYDNEY • AUCKLAND

CONTENTS

THE POWER OF SPORT

There are around eight billion people on the planet and almost all of them have played or watched some sort of sport in their lives. Whoever you are, wherever you come from and whatever language you speak, sport has the power to unite us all.

From cheering on your local football team to a whole nation coming together to support their athletes at the Olympics, we love sport because it makes us feel big emotions. Sport can be thrilling and exhausting to play, and dramatic and mind-blowing to watch! Your own team-mates can become a sort of second family. Stars become heroes. Watching your favourite football team can make you jump for joy or it can ruin your day.

Not only is sport great for your physical and mental health, it gives us incredible role models. These people use their superstar status as a platform to speak about important real-life issues away from the pitch, pool and track. In this book, you will discover people who have excelled in a huge range of sports. From football, rugby and cricket to gymnastics, tennis and boxing, you will find out about how people have used their special talents to make the world a better place for themselves and for others.

CHANGE THE GAME

The twenty sportspeople in this book have not only done amazing things in their chosen sport, but also changed the world for the rest of us. In these stories, we look at the issues they have faced and how they have overcome them to grow as people and in turn help others. This is the true power of sport.

Some of the people in this book are international stars, and others are not as well known. But every one of them has a super sport power. You will read about Marcus Rashford playing football for Manchester United while also tackling the issue of food poverty. You'll learn all about Tegla Loroupe who runs marathons to help stop violence.

They have done great things because they know that sport can make a difference. It can be changing the wider world or just changing how you view it. After reading about these stars and their super sport powers, perhaps you too will be inspired to help others. Inside are twenty different activities to get you started on your journey. This book shows that sport can make the world a better place. Are you ready to be empowered? On your marks, get set … GO!

MEGAN RAPINOE *(b. 1985)*

“BE MORE. BE BETTER. BE BIGGER THAN YOU’VE EVER BEEN BEFORE.”

Megan has helped highlight racism in America. Before a game in 2016, she knelt during the national anthem to show support for Colin Kaepernick. He was an NFL player who had been criticized for kneeling to protest against racial injustice.

Megan is the USA football team's star striker. She helped the USA to win the World Cup in 2015 and 2019 and the Olympic gold medal in 2012. She is the first footballer, male or female, to score a goal directly from a corner at the Olympic Games. She has done this twice! In 2019 she was named one of FIFA's Players of the Year alongside Lionel Messi.

Football helped Megan escape problems growing up. When she became famous, she used her profile to speak out about issues she cares about. She wants everyone to have an equal chance in life, regardless of their sex, gender or race. She is gay and said it was wrong that other players did not feel safe enough to come out and be themselves. She starred in a video to combat name-calling and has even clashed with the President of the USA over the issues she feels strongly about.

She called for the USA women's team to be paid the same as the male team, joining with her team-mates to challenge the organization that makes the rules. Her message to women is simple: "Don't settle for anything less, go for equal, go for more..."

ACTIVITY

WRITE YOUR OWN FAIRNESS PLEDGE

Think of something that you would like to change to make the world a fairer place for everyone. For example it could be: "I believe women should be treated the same as men." Write or draw it on a piece of paper and use it to inspire your friends and family.

SUPER SPORT POWER
BOLDNESS

Megan has always been bold. She did not care if she upset people in power as she fought for equality. Her powerful words about equal pay and other areas of social justice brought her into conflict with politicians, but Megan's strength of character meant she never took a backwards step.

FAIR PLAY

Megan believes everyone should be treated equally. When the USA won the World Cup in 2015 the women's team was paid only a quarter of what the men got, even though they were much more successful. This is unfair, but trailblazers like Megan are refusing to let it happen anymore.

MUHAMMAD ALI *(1942–2016)*

“I SHOOK UP THE WORLD.”

Cassius Clay, as Muhammad was then called, was born in the USA at a time when many Black Americans didn't have the same rights and opportunities as white people. When he was twelve years old, he had his bicycle stolen and said he wanted to “whup” the thief. A policeman told him that if that was his plan then he had better learn how to fight. He went on to become the most famous boxer in history.

In 1960, when he was eighteen, Muhammad won the Olympic gold medal. But despite his triumph, he faced racist abuse and was refused service in a restaurant in his home city because of his skin colour. He reacted by throwing his gold medal in the Ohio River. This was one of many examples in his career where he stood up against racial injustice.

He became the world heavyweight champion when he was just 22. After converting to Islam and changing his name, he became known as Muhammad Ali. Throughout his career, Muhammad never forgot the obstacles he had overcome and gave huge amounts of money to charity and promoted education for young people and the rights of disadvantaged people all over the world.

SUPER SPORT POWER

BELIEF

Muhammad admitted he was terrified about fighting the great champion Sonny Liston for the world title between 1964–65, but by constantly telling himself that he was the greatest and he was going to win, he finally started to believe it.

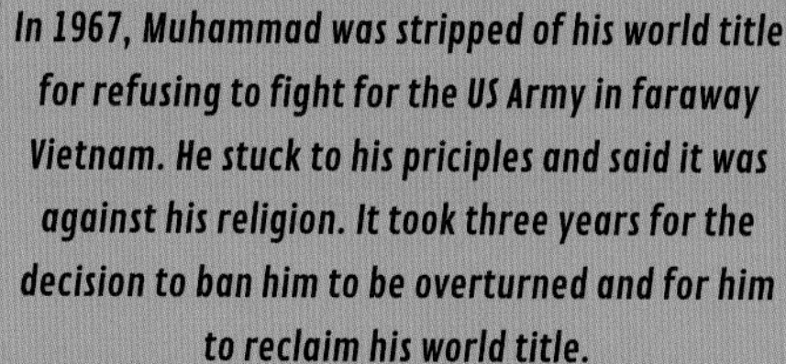

In 1967, Muhammad was stripped of his world title for refusing to fight for the US Army in faraway Vietnam. He stuck to his priciples and said it was against his religion. It took three years for the decision to ban him to be overturned and for him to reclaim his world title.

ACTIVITY

WHO IS THE GREATEST?

Muhammad Ali called himself the Greatest Of All Time. His greatness went well beyond the boxing ring and towards making the world a better place. Which sportsperson do you think is the GOAT in fighting for fairness? Write down their name or draw their picture.

FAIR PLAY

When Muhammad was growing up in the USA, white people had all the power. Segregation laws meant people were divided by their skin colour. Black people were forced to go to different schools, toilets and restaurants to white people. The Civil Rights movement of the 1950s and 60s wanted to end this injustice and ensure everyone was treated equally.

TOM DALEY *(b. 1994)*

"OTHER PEOPLE'S OPINIONS ARE NOT WORTH LOSING SLEEP OVER."

ACTIVITY

CELEBRATE BRILLIANT YOU

We are all different and we should celebrate and respect this. Write down three special things that make you the unique person you are and share them with your friends.

Tom's biggest fan was his dad, Rob, who became seriously ill with a brain tumour. He died the year before the 2012 Olympic Games, when Tom was only seventeen leaving him behind with his mum and brothers. Tom said it made him realize there were more important things than success.

In 2008, when he was only fourteen, Tom competed for Great Britain in diving at the Olympic Games. His fame caused bullies to pick on him at school, but he carried on competing.

Tom's sport is dangerous. He had to climb to the top of a 10-metre platform, the height of a two-storey house, and then dive into a pool while performing a series of somersaults and turns. Away from sport, Tom has shown great bravery in his personal life. Although he became an inspiration to millions after he came out as LGBTQ+ in a video in 2013, some people used social media to bully him for being gay.

Tom is married to Dustin Lance Black and they have a family together, which increased the abuse he received on social media. He didn't let the bullies affect his performance and in 2021, he won his first Olympic gold medal in the 10m synchro alongside his team-mate Matty Lee. Afterwards, he said he was proud to be an Olympic champion and a gay man. He told young LGBTQ+ people that no matter how alone they might feel, they could achieve anything.

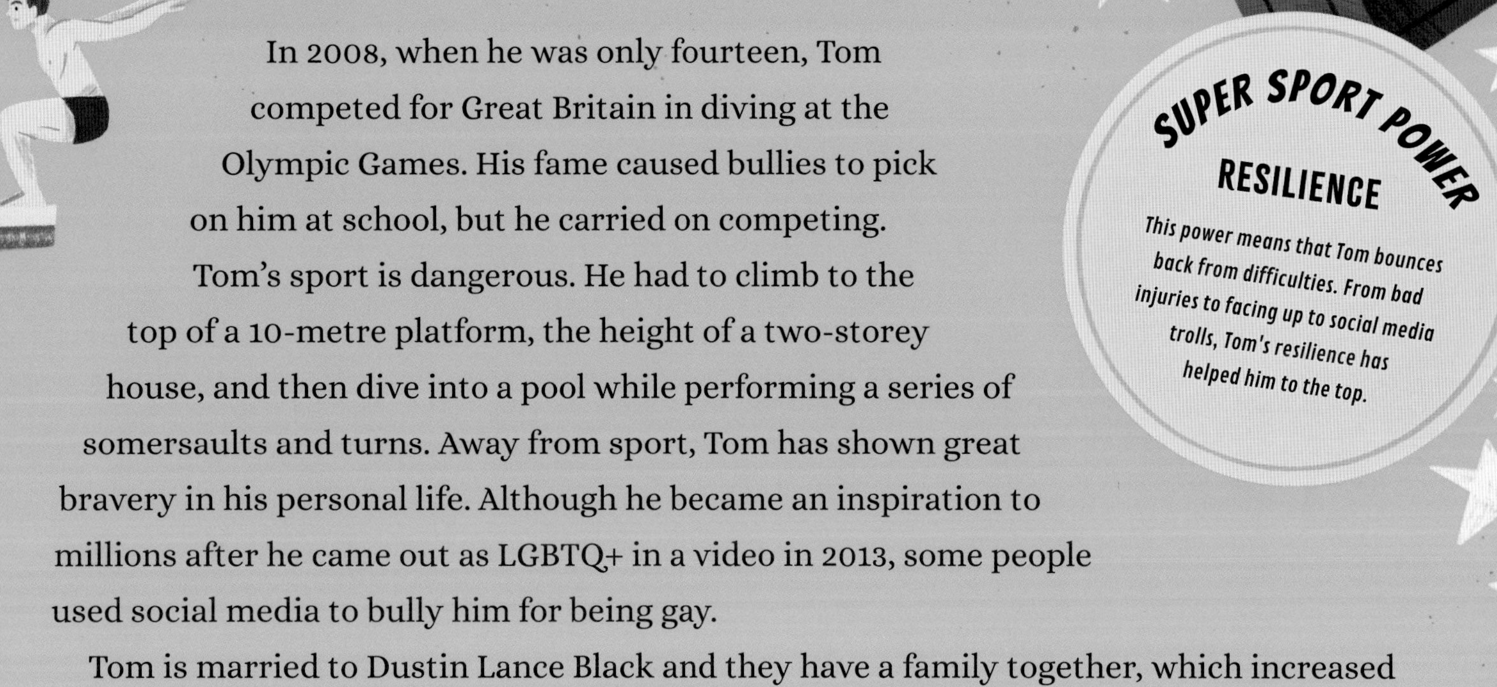

SUPER SPORT POWER

RESILIENCE

This power means that Tom bounces back from difficulties. From bad injuries to facing up to social media trolls, Tom's resilience has helped him to the top.

FAIR PLAY

LGBTQ+ stands for lesbian, gay, bisexual, transgender and queer or questioning and is used by people to explain how they live and love. Being LGBTQ+ is still illegal in some countries. Tom has called for these countries to change their laws so everyone can be themselves and live their lives free from fear and inequality.

LUDWIG GUTTMANN *(1899–1980)*

"I DREAM OF THE DAY WHEN THERE WILL BE AN OLYMPIC GAMES FOR PEOPLE WITH DISABILITIES."

Ludwig was a doctor living in Germany during the Second World War. He was Jewish which meant he and his family were in danger because the leader of Nazi Germany, Adolf Hitler, hated Jews. By 1939, the situation was so bad that Ludwig had to leave.

He ended up in England where he set up the National Spinal Injuries Centre at Stoke Mandeville to help wounded soldiers. Ludwig believed that sport was an important part of their treatment and on the same day that the Olympic Games opened in London in 1948, he organized the first Stoke Mandeville Games. Initially, all the athletes were wounded veterans in wheelchairs, but the event grew to embrace people with many different impairments.

In 1960, Ludwig got his wish of staging his games alongside the Olympic Games in Rome. The first Paralympics featured 400 athletes from 23 countries. Since then, they have taken place every four years and they have inspired millions globally, showing off the talents of brilliant disabled sports stars.

The word "Paralympic" comes from the Greek word "para", which means beside or alongside, and the word "Olympic". It means that the Paralympics are parallel to the Olympic Games and illustrates how both competitions exist side-by-side.

SUPER SPORT POWER

EMPATHY

Empathy is being able to see the world through other people's eyes. Ludwig was able to see things from the point of view of the injured airmen he was treating and realize what they needed to help their rehabilitation.

ACTIVITY

CREATE AN ATHLETE FACT FILE

Make a fact-file about your favourite Paralympic athlete. Research facts about their life and sport, including their achievements or medals. Finish your fact file by drawing a picture of the athlete.

FAIR PLAY

In the past disabled people have been shunned and not given opportunities because of fear and prejudice. Ludwig's Paralympics have helped make people aware of those with impairments. Although there is a long way to go before disabled people are treated equally, the Games have shown that an impairment doesn't stop a person from leading a fulfilled, active and successful life.

EMMA RADUCANU (b. 2002)

"THE CONFIDENCE COMES FROM INNER BELIEF."

In 2021, when she was eighteen, Emma did her final A-level exams at school. Immediately after, she was given the chance to play at Wimbledon, which is one of the biggest tennis tournaments in the world. The organizers wanted to give the young British player some experience, but she astounded everyone by winning three matches. Then she suffered breathing difficulties and had to pull out of her next match, prompting some people to say she needed to "toughen up" and had been overwhelmed by nerves.

Emma was born in Canada. Her mother is Chinese and her father is Romanian, and they moved to England when Emma was two. She speaks three languages: English, Mandarin and Romanian. She is proud of her mixed heritage and who she is.

Two months later, Emma won three qualifying matches to make it to the first round of the US Open, another huge tournament. This time there was no stopping her. She went all the way to the final and beat Leylah Fernandez without dropping a single set.

She was celebrated as a great British star but also made sure she thanked her Chinese fans in Mandarin on YouTube. She hopes her success will cross borders and inspire other young tennis players all over the world.

Emma had to show incredible commitment to reach the top while studying for her A-Levels. She had coaching sessions before starting school at 8.45am. Not long after her win in 2021, she found out she achieved brilliant results in her exams.

SUPER SPORT POWER

IMAGINATION

If you don't believe in miracles, they will not come true. Almost nobody thought someone as inexperienced as Emma could win the US Open, but she had the imagination to picture one of sport's greatest achievements before it happened.

ACTIVITY

merci

Ευχαριστώ

danke

LEARN ANOTHER LANGUAGE

شكرا

谢谢

Emma can speak fluent English and Mandarin and also knows Romanian. Her fans love that she is multilingual. Can you learn to say and write "Thank You" in three different languages?

תודה!

thank you

gracias

FAIR PLAY

Mental health is our emotional wellbeing. Stressful or intense situations can make you feel nervous or worried. It is important to look after our minds as well as our bodies. Sportspeople can often face a lot of pressure which is bad for their mental health. Emma prioritized her mental health and took a break to look after herself and went on to win the US Open.

SIMONE BILES *(b. 1997)*

"YOU WILL NOT ALWAYS BE STRONG, BUT YOU CAN ALWAYS BE BRAVE."

Nobody expected Simone to be a star when she was growing up. Her parents couldn't look after her so she lived with a foster family. Simone's life changed one day when she tried gymnastics and discovered she was a natural.

Gymnastics is tough and Simone was injured many times on the way to the top. She also faced racism for being one of the few Black USA gymnasts. At just 4 feet 8 inches tall, she was also bullied for being small. But when she was only nineteen, she won a staggering four gold medals at the 2016 Olympic Games.

In 2018, she became ill at the World Championships in Qatar. She was forced to go to hospital, but she did not want to let her team down, so she checked out of hospital and the next day helped the USA win the gold medal.

Simone has always been incredibly brave. She became the first woman to perform the dangerous triple-double somersault in a competition. She showed even more courage when she spoke out about a coach who had bullied and hurt her and her team-mates. The coach went to jail and Simone became a hero for others who have suffered at the hands of bullies.

SUPER SPORT POWER

COURAGE

Simone needs courage to do somersaults high in the air, but she also needed it to speak out about her coach's abusive nature. It put her in the spotlight and was difficult for her, but she knew she would be helping others.

In 2021, Simone bravely admitted she was suffering from a crisis of confidence at the Olympic Games. Her mental health was suffering from the pressure of competing. She withdrew from five events but made a heroic return and won a bronze medal on the balance beam.

FAIR PLAY

Bullying is unkind behaviour that hurts someone else. Simone was bullied by other children at school because of her appearance and by people on the internet who would criticize her and say mean things. It is never OK to make someone feel bad about themselves and Simone bravely opened up about what was happening to her.

ACTIVITY

MAKE A KINDNESS PLEDGE

We all have the power to choose how we treat others. A pledge is a promise. Think of three acts of kindness you can pledge to help stop bullying.

IBTIHAJ MUHAMMAD *(b. 1985)*

"WHEN WE STAND IN SOLIDARITY, WE'LL BE STRONGER."

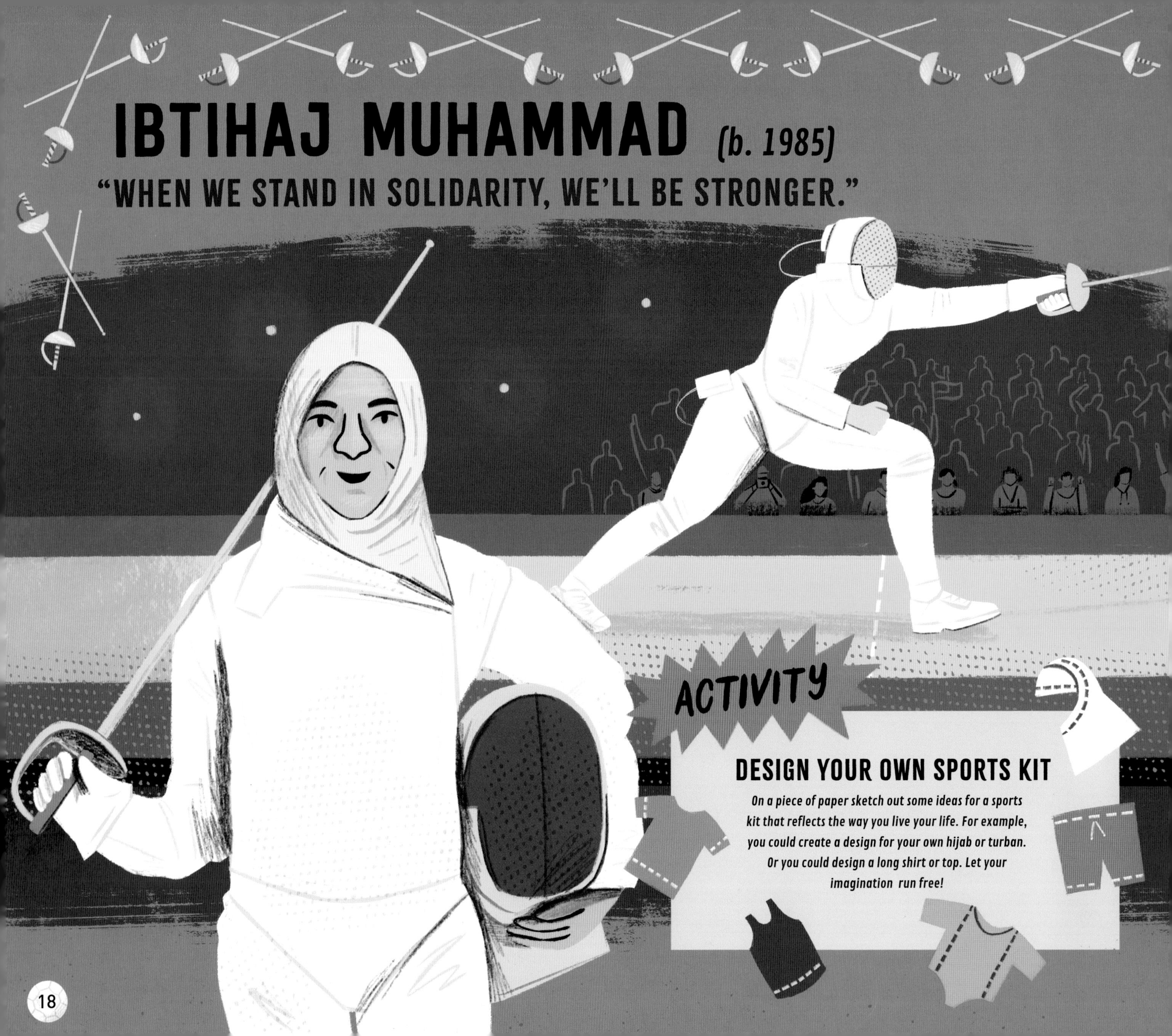

ACTIVITY

DESIGN YOUR OWN SPORTS KIT

On a piece of paper sketch out some ideas for a sports kit that reflects the way you live your life. For example, you could create a design for your own hijab or turban. Or you could design a long shirt or top. Let your imagination run free!

Growing up in the USA, Ibtihaj wore a headscarf called a hijab, which Muslim women wear to cover their hair. Ibtihaj's parents wanted her to take up a sport which allowed her to cover her body according to the rules of Islam, so she began fencing. Ibtihaj didn't see many sports stars who looked like her and this made her unique, fencing as a Muslim wearing a hijab. In 2001, terrorists associated with an extreme Islamist group attacked the USA which led to an increase in hate crimes against Muslims. Ibtihaj did not let this set her back or stop her from wearing her hijab. She said she wanted to make her sport and American society more inclusive, so people realized that everyone is the same even if their religions are different.

Ibtihaj was a five-time senior world medallist and in 2016 was the first American woman to compete in a hijab and the first American-Muslim woman to win a bronze medal at the Olympic Games. By wearing her hijab while competing and speaking out about her experiences, she helped break down harmful beliefs about Muslims.

SUPER SPORT POWER

BEING YOURSELF

It is easy to go along with the crowd and want to fit in. Sometimes, though, it is important to do what Ibtihaj did and stand out and be true to yourself.

FAIR PLAY

Islam is the world's second largest religion, and its followers are called Muslims. Some people refuse to accept that Islam is a peaceful religion and their hostile views have become known as Islamophobia. In the face of prejudice, Ibtihaj has fought for the opportunity to play sport regardless of her faith.

Ibtihaj's influence beyond sport was shown when a famous toy company made a Barbie doll of her wearing her hijab in celebration of women who break boundaries.

LEBRON JAMES (b. 1984)

"MY PAIN WAS MOTIVATION."

After Jacob Blake, a Black man, was shot by a policeman in 2020, LeBron and his LA Lakers team-mates refused to play in the NBA play-offs in protest.

ACTIVITY

MAKE YOUR VOICE HEARD

Write a letter or an email to someone in power about an issue that you feel strongly about. You could write to your teacher, headteacher or local politician about something you want to change for the better, such as racial injustice.

LeBron had a tough upbringing in Ohio, USA. His mother, Gloria Marie, worked tirelessly to provide for him, but money was tight and they had to move many times. Finally, it was decided LeBron would have better opportunities if he went to live with a local sports coach called Frank Walker.

Frank introduced LeBron to basketball when he was nine and he would go on to become a huge star with the Cleveland Cavaliers, Miami Heat and LA Lakers. He was a four-time NBA champion between 2012 and 2020 and 18-time NBA All-Star, scoring more than 35,000 points. Many people consider him the greatest player of all time, but LeBron never forgot how hard it had been growing up and wanted to use his fame to help others.

LeBron built a school for poor children in his hometown, donated $2.5m to fund an exhibition about his Civil Rights hero, Muhammad Ali, and became a leading supporter of the Black Lives Matter movement.

Realizing that lasting change needed to come from politicians, LeBron urged more Black Americans to vote in the Presidential election. His willingness to speak out against injustice attracted criticism, but LeBron refused to be silent.

SUPER SPORT POWER

LEADERSHIP

LeBron has not always played in the best team, but he has always tried to the best he can. He takes the lead whilst making those around him better.

FAIR PLAY

In 2020 there were worldwide protests against racial injustice after a Black man named George Floyd died while in police custody. LeBron, and other sports stars, spoke out in support of the Black Lives Matter movement which aims to stop violence against Black communities.

HUSNAH KUKUNDAKWE *(b. 2007)*

"THIS IS THE START OF MY JOURNEY."

Husnah was born without the lower part of her right arm and an impairment to her left hand. In Uganda, the African country where she lived, disabled children were often abandoned by their parents. Many were forced to live on the street.

At school people would look at Husnah differently and some people would laugh at her. Even if it was hot, she would wear a baggy jumper so she could hide her impairment. Then, one day, she tried swimming and loved it. Husnah got used to jumping in the pool, which raised her confidence and stopped her feeling shy. Even though a teacher replaced her in a competition with a swimmer who was able-bodied, Husnah didn't let it shake her new-found confidence.

In 2021, aged just fourteen, Husnah went to the Paralympics in Tokyo. She was the youngest competitor out of over 4,400 athletes and the only Paralympic swimmer from Uganda.

Husnah said that her appearance at the Paralympics was just the beginning. "I feel like I can touch the clouds," she said after finishing sixth in her heat. She said her new goal was to win a medal in Paris in 2024.

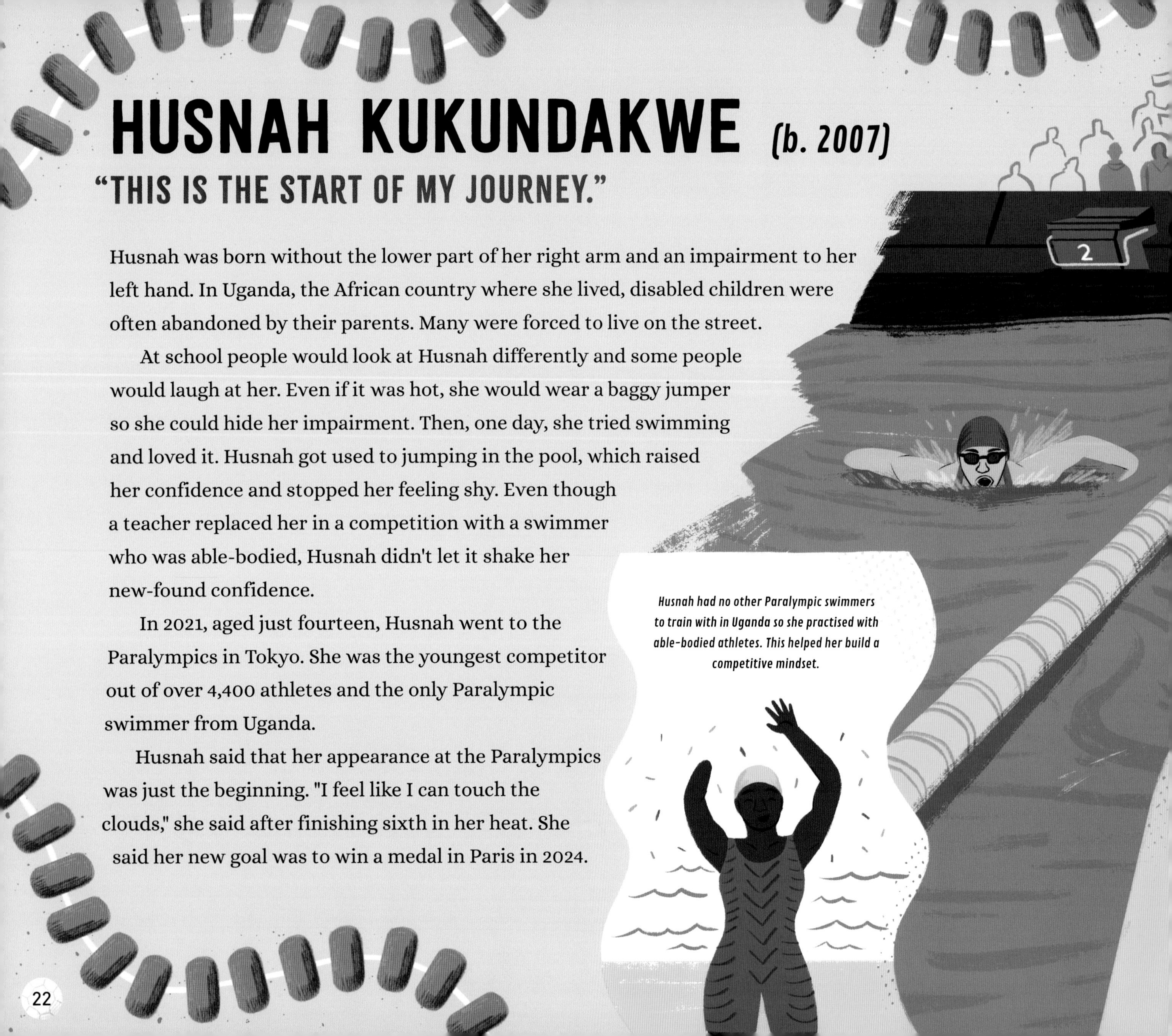

Husnah had no other Paralympic swimmers to train with in Uganda so she practised with able-bodied athletes. This helped her build a competitive mindset.

SUPER SPORT POWER

BRAVERY

Everyone feels fear, but it is how we deal with it that matters. The more you hide from a problem the bigger it feels. Husnah faced her fear by taking off her jumper and realizing she could deal with people staring at her.

FAIR PLAY

In international sport, there is something called the "disability divide". This means it is harder for disabled athletes in some countries to get opportunities to compete. This can be down to a lack of money for equipment like racing wheelchairs or it can be down to prejudice against disabled people.

ACTIVITY

DESIGN YOUR OWN PARALYMPIC MEDAL

Design a medal for the Paralympic Games. Make your design reflect the values you think are most important in the Games.

PALWANKAR BALOO *(1876–1955)*

“AN EXTRAORDINARY CRICKETER WHO BATTLED INCREDIBLE DISCRIMINATION.” – *RAMACHANDRA GUHA, HISTORIAN*

SUPER SPORT POWER

CONFIDENCE

Palwankar knew he could rely on his cricketing ability and that gave him confidence to battle against the odds. His confidence enabled him to make lasting change.

Palwankar started out working as a groundsman at a cricket club in Pune in India, but soon showed real talent as a bowler. He was a Hindu and belonged to the lowest group, or caste, in Indian society. Because of his low caste, he wasn't allowed to play cricket.

But Palwankar was so good that the Hindu team wanted him to play for them. However, he did not have the same rights as the other players. When the team had lunch during a match, Palwankar had to eat at a separate table and he was only allowed to drink from a plastic cup.

In 1911, India sent a team to tour in England and, although they lost, Palwankar played brilliantly and took an incredible 114 wickets. He was celebrated all over India but especially by the lower classes who saw him as an inspiration. So when Palwankar was not selected to play for the Hindu team in the important Bombay Quadrangular Tournament, there was an outcry and the selectors had to change their minds.

Palwankar later became a politician and supported Mahatma Gandhi's fight to end British rule in India. He showed that a person's level of education or wealth should have no bearing on how well they are treated by society.

FAIR PLAY

For many years, Indian Hindus were divided into four different social groups called castes. Palwankar was part of a fifth group called Dalits. They were known as outcasts because they didn't belong to any of the main castes. Each group would stick together and do similar jobs. This is now changing in modern India and society is becoming fairer for all.

ACTIVITY

TAKE THE MILLION POUND CHALLENGE

Imagine if you had a million pounds. It is a lot of money! Now imagine you could use it to help people in society who are less fortunate than you and make things fairer. Write down three things you would do with the money, such as founding a new type of sports club that is for everyone to use.

Despite his brilliance, Palwankar was never made captain of the Hindu team because of his lower caste. Between 1910–20 there was a campaign to make him captain but it was always unsuccessful. Years later, his brother Palwankar Vithal was made captain and that had a big impact on social change in India.

ELLEN MACARTHUR *(b. 1976)*

"COURAGE IS NOT HAVING THE ENERGY TO GO ON; IT'S GOING ON WHEN YOU DO NOT HAVE THE ENERGY."

SUPER SPORT POWER

OPEN-MINDEDNESS

People who are open-minded are willing to see challenges as opportunities. Ellen was a famous sailor but decided she wanted to take on a new challenge and do something to help the planet.

When Ellen MacArthur read a book about boats called *Swallows and Amazons*, she knew she wanted to become a sailor. At primary school she started saving money to buy her first small boat.

When she was eighteen, she sailed around the coast of Great Britain on her own. Then when she was 24, she became the youngest sailor to complete the round-the-world race called the Vendée Globe. Four years later she became an international star when she became the fastest person to sail non-stop around the world on her own. She covered over 26,000 miles in 71 days and discovered you can survive on very little food, water and fuel.

After retiring from racing, she set up the Ellen MacArthur Foundation to create new ways of recycling to help reduce waste and pollution. She knew from sailing that if you use up your supplies too quickly, then your race will be a disaster. She believes the same is true of the planet and that we need to take great care not to use up the world's resources too quickly. Ellen spoke to environment experts, politicians and companies and created a network of people striving to save the planet.

ACTIVITY

PLAY LITTER LOTTO

With a group of friends draw pictures of six pieces of litter you often see in your local area. Every time you pick up one of the items and put it in a recycling bin, cross it off your card. The first person to get all the items is the winner.

FAIR PLAY

Plastic in the ocean is harmful to wildlife, as they become tangled in it or become ill after swallowing it. By 2050, experts predict there will be more pieces of plastic in the sea than fish. Ellen wants people to think about how things can be continually reused rather than thrown away.

Ellen had not planned on giving up sailing but realized her new fame gave her an opportunity to make lasting change. She remembered writing: "What I have got on the boat is everything." At sea sailors took care of every item, but on dry land people wasted so much.

MEL YOUNG (b. 1953)

"I'M IN. ARE YOU?"

SUPER SPORT POWER

AMBITION

There is a saying: "Aim for the moon and even if you fall short you will still reach the stars." Ambition gives us a goal and a purpose. Mel thought big when he decided to create a new World Cup.

When Mel Young was studying at university in Scotland, he became aware that many people in the city were homeless. They were forced to sleep on the cold streets. This was dangerous and affected their mental health.

One day at a conference in Austria, Mel and his friend Harald Schmied came up with the idea of using football to help homeless people change their own lives. They believed that bringing people together to play in a football tournament would make them feel part of a community and create a sense of purpose and achievement, as well as encouraging healthy living. They also wanted to shine a light on a problem that was often ignored by governments.

The first Homeless World Cup took place in Austria in 2003 and since then it has been held in countries all over the world. Games can be anything from two to 20-a-side and there are prizes for all skills and levels. Players say that being part of the tournament changed their lives and people who attend say it made them think differently about homelessness.

FAIR PLAY

Millions of people around the world are homeless. This could be because of a lack of housing, an unexpected life event or prejudice. Those without a home are often lonely and struggle with poor physical and mental health. Mel wants to challenge the negative way some people think about those living on the streets.

ACTIVITY

HELP THE HOMELESS

You can raise money to help the homeless. Find out where your local shelter is. You could hold a sponsored silence or walk at your school to raise money for it or donate items that the shelter needs.

Mel co-founded *The Big Issue* in Scotland. *The Big Issue* is a magazine sold by homeless and vulnerable people so they can support themselves by earning money. The magazine has now been published for over 30 years and sold over 200 million copies.

TEGLA LOROUPE *(b. 1973)*

"SPORTS CAN CREATE PEACE."

Growing up in Kenya, Tegla worked in the fields, looked after cattle and was told that the best she could dream of was looking after her younger brothers and sisters. But she had to run ten kilometres to school each morning and her amazing running ability was soon spotted. Despite not having the support of her father, she started racing. When she won a prestigious cross-country race at the age of fifteen, she was on her way to becoming a star.

At that point there had been many famous male runners in Kenya. Tegla was the first Kenyan woman to break through when she became the first female African athlete to win the New York City Marathon in 1994. Four years later she broke the marathon world record. She became a celebrity in Kenya and a hero to countless young athletes.

Tegla never forgot what it was like growing up among local conflicts between different tribes over cattle. She wanted to give something back to her community so set up a Peace Marathon, which encouraged thousands of local warriors from different tribes to lay down their weapons and run together. She also works with refugees, by helping children to continue their education and by training athletes in refugee camps.

In 2016 and 2021 Tegla went to the Olympic Games as the chief of the Refugee Team. The Refugee Team was made up of athletes who had been forced to leave their homelands due to wars or their lives being in danger.

SUPER SPORT POWER

FAITH

Many people thought you could never stop enemies fighting each other, but Tegla was not one of those. She had faith in the underlying goodness of people and knew that her Peace Marathons could make society better.

ACTIVITY

DO YOUR OWN CHARITY RACE

Choose a cause you would like to raise money for and plan a charity race with your friends. You can decide the distance and you could run, walk, skip or scoot it! Ask people to sponsor you to complete the distance.

FAIR PLAY

Tegla created the Tegla Loroupe Peace Foundation to promote peace through sport and highlight the suffering of refugees. When she visited refugee camps, she met people who had to leave their homes and had lost everything. She wanted to give them hope and opportunity so she petitioned the Olympic committee to create a team of refugees.

SAEID MOLLAEI *(b. 1992)*

"I JUST WANT TO BE COURAGEOUS AND LIVE FREELY."

In 2021, Saeid caused a storm when he decided to train in Israel before the Olympic Games. He dedicated his subsequent medal to Israel, showing that people are free to make their own choices.

Saeid Mollaei grew up in Iran, a country that for many years had been locked in bitter conflict with nearby Israel. Since 1979, Iranian sportspeople had not been allowed to compete against Israelis in international competitions.

Saeid was brilliant at judo, and when he was 23, he won a bronze medal at the Asian Championships. He continued to improve and by 2018 he was the world champion and a star in Iran. Then his life changed dramatically. At the 2019 World Championships in Tokyo, Iranian sporting chiefs and politicians demanded that Saeid deliberately lose a match to avoid having to take on the Israeli champion, Sagi Muki, in the finals. Saeid thought a political row between two countries had nothing to do with his sport and refused. When he then lost in the tournament, he went public and explained why the politicians were wrong to interfere in sport.

Fearing for his life if he went back to Iran, Saeid fled to Germany where he became a refugee and then gained Mongolian citizenship. In 2021, Saeid went back to Tokyo for the Olympic Games and won a silver medal for Mongolia. He also competed in Israel where he met Sagi Muki again. They talked of how sport could bring people together and the two are now friends.

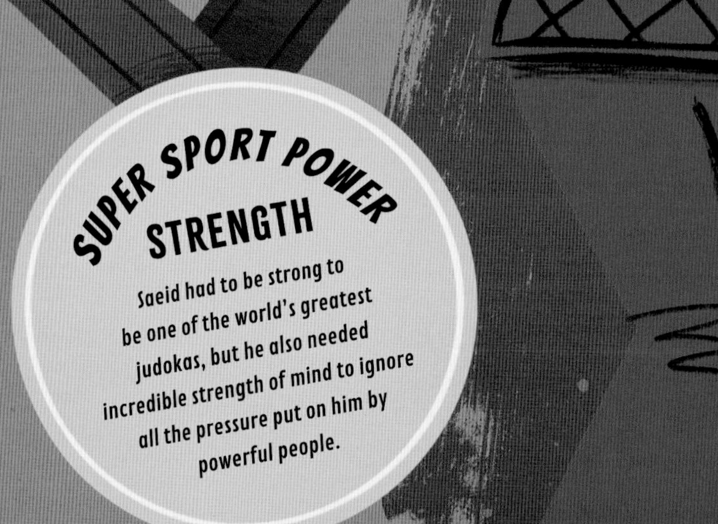

SUPER SPORT POWER

STRENGTH

Saeid had to be strong to be one of the world's greatest judokas, but he also needed incredible strength of mind to ignore all the pressure put on him by powerful people.

FAIR PLAY

Saeid is one example of how sportspeople around the world have faced terrible danger from making a political stand. Sportspeople bring a lot of attention to their countries and sometimes governments try to use them to make themselves more popular. Governments can also be scared that the sportspeople might use their fame to speak out against their policies. Making a stand can take enormous courage.

ACTIVITY

TAKE CHARGE OF WORLD SPORT

Imagine you have got a new job as the World Sports Minister. You have the power to change anything in sport. Choose three things. It might be cheaper tickets, longer games or more opportunities.

CATHY FREEMAN *(b. 1973)*

"I COULD NEVER UNDERSTAND WHY I SMILED AT SOMEONE, AND THEY NEVER SMILED BACK."

SUPER SPORT POWER

PRIDE

Knowing who you are and what you stand for means you can overcome negativity. Proud of her heritage, Cathy knew she was running for indigenous people all over the world.

When Cathy was fourteen her dream was to win an Olympic gold medal. She was only sixteen when she won a gold medal in the relay at the 1990 Commonwealth Games. Four years later she won the 200m and 400m gold medals at the same event in Canada. Cathy was proud of her indigenous roots, and she celebrated with both the Australia and Australian aboriginal flags. Although lots of people supported her for that, many of those in power condemned her.

By the time the 2000 Olympic Games were held in Australia, Cathy was an international star. Cathy knew that she was running for more than a medal. In the Opening Ceremony, she lit the Olympic flame. Wearing a hooded green and white bodysuit, she then produced a jaw-dropping run to win the 400m gold medal. Although celebrating with the Australian Aboriginal flag was not officially permitted at the Olympic Games, Cathy proudly flew it as she ran her victory lap. Afterwards she said her ancestors had been the first to walk this land and that she had felt protected by them during the race.

Cathy retired from racing in 2003 and has spent much of her life trying to improve education opportunities for indigenous people.

ACTIVITY

START A FAMILY TREE

Create a family tree by asking your parents, grandparents, aunts and uncles about their ancestors. Write down their names, dates of birth and a fact about them if you know them.

FAIR PLAY

Indigenous people are descendants of the first inhabitants of a country, before settlers arrived. In Australia, the Aboriginal people and Torres Strait Islanders had their lands stolen by European settlers. For hundreds of years, they were treated cruelly by the government and children were even taken away from their families. Cathy showed that all Australians deserved equal freedoms and rights.

Four years after her gold medal triumph and after she had flown the Australian Aboriginal flag, Cathy was given the honour of carrying the Oceania flag, representing her entire continent at the Opening Ceremony of the 2004 Olympic Games.

BILLY MONGER *(b. 1999)*

"I DON'T HAVE TIME FOR SELF-PITY."

The rain was pouring down on the Donington Park racetrack in 2017, as seventeen-year-old Billy Monger competed in the British Formula 4 Championship. The conditions meant the boy nicknamed "Billy Whizz" did not see the stationary car in front of him until it was too late. He crashed into it at 120mph.

Billy's injuries were so bad that he was put in a coma and had to have both of his legs amputated. That might have been the end of his motor-racing career, but Billy wanted to return to the sport he loved. Famous Formula One drivers and fans were all moved by his courage and helped raise money to help him get better. Billy's team built a new car with the brakes and throttle on the steering wheel, so he did not have to use his legs to drive. Billy also made the people in charge of motorsport change their rules to allow disabled drivers to race in single-seater cars.

To everyone's amazement Billy was back in a car just eleven weeks after his accident. He became the first-ever double amputee to race competitively in a single-seater racing car, at just eighteen years of age. He now wants to win more races while raising awareness about disabilities in sport.

SUPER SPORT POWER
POSITIVITY

Billy always stayed positive and cheerful despite the odds being against him. He felt things would get better even after losing his legs. Without that attitude he would never have had the enthusiasm to race again.

ACTIVITY

HOLD A FUNDRAISING CHALLENGE

Think of different ways you could raise money for a cause. You could hold a garden sale to sell old clothes and toys, a bake sale or a sponsored fancy dress event.

FAIR PLAY

Ableism is discrimination against people because they have a disability. Disabled people face many challenges such as gaining equal opportunities and better access to places the non-disabled take for granted. Billy had to fight to change motor-racing rules so he could compete with able-bodied drivers.

In 2021, Billy did a charity triathlon over four days, which was made up of an 18-mile kayak, 26.2-mile run and 95-mile bike ride. He raised more than £2 million for charity.

MARIA TOORPAKAI *(b. 1990)*

"GIRLS CAN BE ANYTHING IF YOU GIVE THEM A CHANCE."

Maria loved to go outside and play, but this put her in danger in the part of Pakistan where she grew up. A violent group called the Taliban controlled the area and girls were meant to stay indoors and not go to school. Girls were not allowed to play sport at all.

Maria decided to dress up like a boy, so she burned her dresses, cut her hair and wore her brother's clothes. She was supported by her parents, who believed girls and boys should be treated equally. First she tried weightlifting, before falling in love with squash.

Eventually, in order to keep training, she had to reveal that she was a girl. Despite turning professional in 2006 and winning lots of matches, the Taliban threatened her and her family. For three years, Maria stayed inside and practised against a wall before she decided it would be safer if she left the country. Finally, she fled to Canada.

Her bravery and resilience helped her rise through the world ranks, but Maria's greatest success was in fighting for the rights of girls and women in Pakistan. She said she wanted to empower them and give them the strength to overcome obstacles like she had.

When Maria decided to dress up as a boy, her father nicknamed her Genghis Khan after a famous warrior. She used this name when she competed in weightlifting competitions.

SUPER SPORT POWER

DETERMINATION

Determination is the ability to keep going despite setbacks. Maria's determination enabled her to find new ways to compete even though it was against the rules.

FAIR PLAY

Maria had to battle sexism throughout her career. Sexism is when you believe one gender is better than another. This can lead to girls and women not being allowed to do the same things as men and boys or even losing their rights. They might not be able to go to school, have a bank account, take part in politics or play sport.

ACTIVITY

DREAM YOUR FUTURE

Without even knowing it, many of us have beliefs and views that we have learned from the world around us. It is important not to let this prejudice affect how we think about ourselves or others. Maria refused to believe that she shouldn't play sport because people in power told her it wasn't for girls. Be inspired by Maria and think about three different things you would like to achieve in your life that you previously might have thought weren't for you. Dream big!

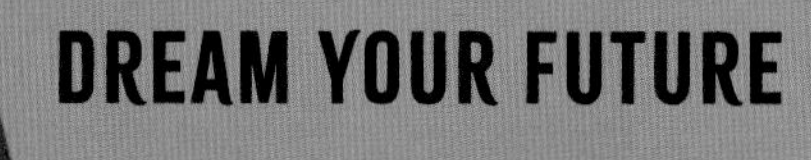

MORNÉ DU PLESSIS *(b. 1949)*

"IT WAS MORE THAN SPORT, BUT SPORT WAS THE STAGE."

In 1980, one of Morné's team-mates died after breaking his neck during a rugby match. Morné set up the Chris Burger Fund to help other players who suffered catastrophic injuries.

When Morné was growing up in South Africa, he excelled at playing rugby, just like his father. He went on to become a very successful captain of the national team, nicknamed the Springboks. In the 1970s, he led them to famous series wins against New Zealand and the British Lions. When Morné travelled to other countries with the Springboks, he witnessed protests against the apartheid system in South African government that unfairly discriminated against Black people. Apartheid meant that Black people weren't allowed to play rugby in South Africa. Morné later said he wished he had spoken up against it earlier.

In 1995, after he had retired, Morné returned as the Springboks' manager. This was a time of great change in South Africa. After years of imprisonment by the South African government, Nelson Mandela, an anti-apartheid campaigner, had become the country's first Black president in 1994.

Morné and Nelson worked together to use the 1995 Rugby World Cup in South Africa to unite the nation. Morné inspired his players to believe in the tournament's slogan: "One team, one country". South Africa won the World Cup against New Zealand in a match that went beyond sport to inspire hope.

SUPER SPORT POWER

TEAM-WORK

Morné had been an international rugby star and knew you could never achieve anything without team-work. By then joining up with Nelson Mandela he helped change deep-seated prejudices in South Africa.

FAIR PLAY

In 1948, the South African government introduced the racist apartheid system, which divided the country. White people had more land, power and money, while Black people had to to live in separate areas and didn't have the right to vote. Apartheid ended in the 1990s, and rugby was a way to unite the country and start healing its deep divisions.

ACTIVITY

MAKE A PROTEST POSTER

Activists in South Africa and around the world bravely protested against apartheid. Make a poster about an issue that matters to you, such as racism or bullying, and think about where you could display it: in your window at home, at school or at your sports club.

SKY BROWN *(b. 2008)*

"IT'S OKAY TO FALL."

Sky Brown always loved skateboarding. Her family were skaters and Sky was competing by the time she was eight and had turned professional by the time she was ten.

She loved skateboarding so much that she refused to give up when she suffered a terrifying accident when she was eleven that left her with a fractured skull and a broken hand. Sky came back and won the gold medal at the prestigious X Games when she became the first female to do a frontside 540, one of the most complicated tricks.

Then came the 2021 Olympic Games when she became the youngest ever athlete to represent Great Britain at the age of 13. With the world watching, she held her nerve to pull off a brilliant final run to make the podium and win a bronze medal.

Sky knew she was lucky to have sporting opportunities and that her skateboarding talent could inspire other children to battle the odds and follow their dreams. She teamed up with a charity which aims to empower all young people, especially in places where there is limited access to education and sport. She helped design boards to be sold for charity and pledged to give children the chance to become leaders for a better world.

SUPER SPORT POWER

COMMITMENT

After her accident, Sky could have thought she was not good enough and given up skateboarding. Instead, she got back on her board and realized failures are just things that help us grow.

Sky grew up in an area without any skate parks and she did not have a coach to teach her. This didn't hold her back though, and she would learn her tricks from watching YouTube videos.

FAIR PLAY

Both older and younger people can be treated unfairly because of their age. Ageism is when someone is told that their opinions don't matter or that they aren't capable or talented enough to do something because of how old they are. Sky showed that age shouldn't be a barrier to competing at the Olympic Games and that competitors should be taken seriously regardless of their age.

ACTIVITY

CREATE AN OLYMPIC SPORT

Skateboarding first featured at the Olympic Games in 2021. What other sports can you think of that should be included? These could be sports that already exist, or they could be ones you've made up.

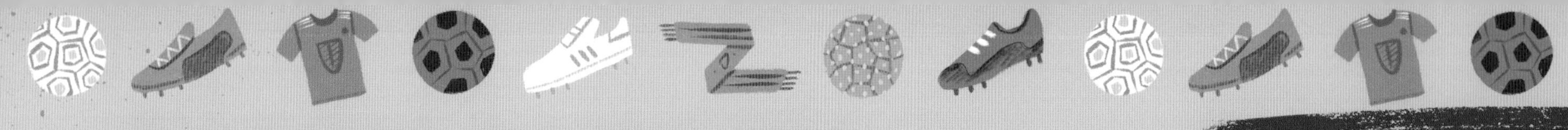

MARCUS RASHFORD *(b. 1997)*

"LOOK AT WHAT WE CAN DO WHEN WE COME TOGETHER."

Marcus became famous playing football. An electric striker, he scored in his first game for his hometown club of Manchester United. He became renowned for his speed, skills and spectacular goals. When he was only eighteen, he was called up to play for England. He became the youngest player in history to score on his debut.

But Marcus wanted to do more than play football. He remembered what it was like growing up when his mother worked very hard but still struggled to provide enough food for her five children. Marcus had free school meals and went to breakfast clubs, and his family used food banks in order to survive.

In 2020, during the Coronavirus pandemic, when schools were closed, Marcus was worried that children like him would not have enough to eat. Marcus started a petition and spoke out on television and social media to make sure that the government supported children. He worked with charities to get food to families that needed it. A million people signed his petition and his campaign raised millions of pounds from the public and businesses.

Now, when he is not playing football for Manchester United and England, Marcus works with charities to make life better for children going through the same things he experienced as a boy.

Marcus was criticized for speaking out about child poverty and people told him to stick to football. He didn't let the negativity affect him on the pitch: at the height of his campaign in 2020, he scored a hat-trick for Manchester United in just 16 minutes in the Champions League.

SUPER SPORT POWER

KINDNESS

Marcus could have been content with being a millionaire superstar, but his kindness towards other people forced him to use his platform to improve their lives.

ACTIVITY

DONATE TO A FOOD BANK

Food banks are places where families can get emergency supplies if they need them. You can leave donations for food banks in supermarkets and community centres. Often there will be a list of essential items that they need. Ask an adult if you can donate an item from the list.

FAIR PLAY

Growing up in poverty means you often lack basic things such as a home or food or clothes. Living in poverty can lead to poor physical and mental health and makes it harder to be a success or reach your full potential. Marcus knows how difficult it is to live in poverty and has campaigned to change things for children in the UK.

NOW IT'S YOUR TURN

So: you have read about Emma, Megan, Husnah, Tom, Billy, Saeid and more. Incredible, aren't they? Now it's down to you. Think about these stories. Which ones most relate to things that are important to you? What qualities have these sportspeople shown that you can use to make the world a better place? Think about what you want to do to achieve your goal – like Marcus, Maria and Ibtihaj, set your targets and then plan your steps.

You've got this!

WHAT ISSUES DO YOU CARE ABOUT?

BULLYING
SEXISM
RACIAL INEQUALITY
POLLUTION
HOMELESSNESS
FOOD POVERTY
CLIMATE CHANGE
DISABILITY
WOMEN'S RIGHTS

HOW TO CHANGE THE GAME

- Think about what you would like to change. This can be a personal thing, like having more confidence and being braver. Or it can be a wider, public issue such as climate change.
- Look at the list of super sport powers. Choose three you already have and three more that you want to improve in order to achieve your goals.

WHAT ARE YOUR SUPER SPORT POWERS?

Boldness	Leadership	Pride
Belief	Bravery	Positivity
Resilience	Confidence	Determination
Empathy	Open-mindedness	Team-work
Imagination	Ambition	Commitment
Courage	Faith	Kindness
Being yourself	Strength	

OTHER BOOKS IN THIS SERIES:

Available from all good booksellers

FOR ROWAN AND BAXTER BROADBENT – R.B.

FOR MOM AND DAD, RALEIGH, AND ZAAK – A.M.

First published 2023 by Walker Books Ltd
87 Vauxhall Walk, London SE11 5HJ

2 4 6 8 10 9 7 5 3 1

This book has been typeset in Alice

Printed in China

British Library Cataloguing in Publication Data: a catalogue record for this book is available from the British Library

Hardback ISBN 978-1-5295-0711-9
Paperback ISBN 978-1-5295-1644-9

www.walker.co.uk